This Book Belongs To:

_____

In the Beginning

In the Beginning

Dandi Daley Mackall

Illustrated by
James Kandt

A Division of Thomas Nelson Publishers
Since 1798

www.thomasnelson.com

Text © 2005 by Dandi Daley Mackall
Illustrations © 2005 by James Kandt

Published in Nashville, Tennessee, by Tommy Nelson®, a Division of Thomas Nelson, Inc.

Scripture quoted from the *International Children's Bible*®, *New Century Version*®, copyright © 1986, 1988, 1999 by Tommy Nelson®, a Division of Thomas Nelson, Inc., Nashville, TN 37214. Used by permission.

Tommy Nelson® books may be purchased in bulk for educational, business, fundraising, or sales promotional use. For information, please e-mail SpecialMarkets@ThomasNelson.com.

ISBN: 1-4003-0525-X

Library of Congress Cataloging-in-Publication Data

Mackall, Dandi Daley.
  In the beginning / Dandi Daley Mackall ; illustrated by James Kandt.
       p. cm.
  ISBN 1-4003-0525-X (hardcover)
  1. Creationism--Juvenile literature.   I. Kandt, James. II. Title.
  BS651.M242 2005
  231.7'65--dc22

                                                      2005014246

Printed in the USA
05 06 07 08 RRD 5 4 3 2 1

I dedicate this book to the memory
of my dad, Frank R. Daley, M.D.,
who gave me a wonderful beginning—
a love for rhythm and rhyme, and more
importantly, a love for God and family.

In the beginning God created the
sky and the earth.
— Genesis 1:1

Before the world began, there was
the Word. The Word was with God,
and the Word was God. He was God
in the beginning. All things were
made through him. Nothing was
made without him.
— John 1:1-3

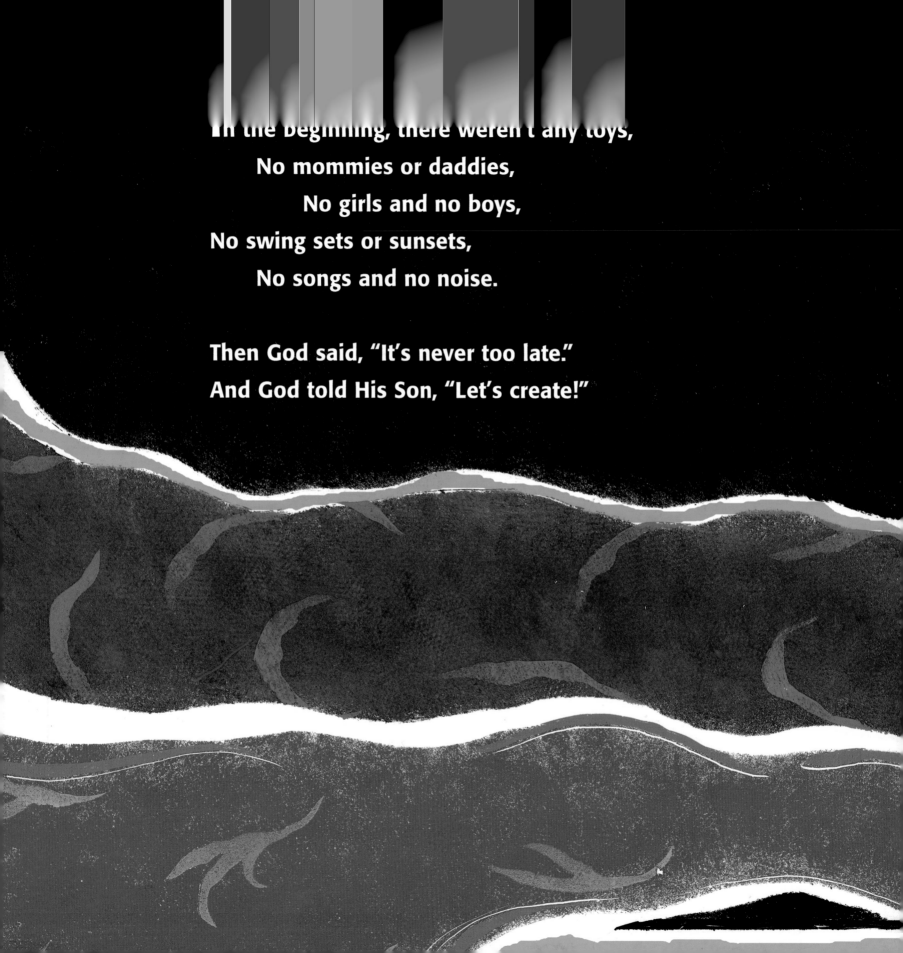

In the beginning, there weren't any toys,
No mommies or daddies,
No girls and no boys,
No swing sets or sunsets,
No songs and no noise.

Then God said, "It's never too late."
And God told His Son, "Let's create!"

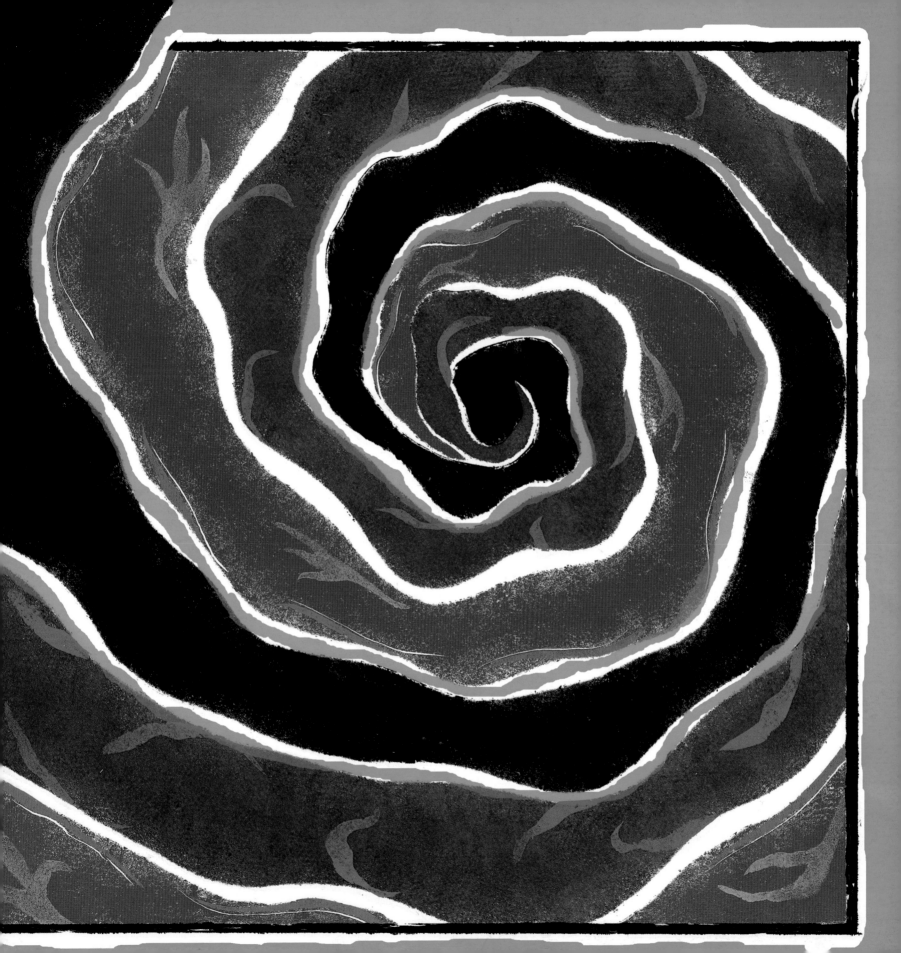

With nothing but darkness, the Lord shouted, "Light!"
And out of pure nothing, God made day and night.
The Father and Son laughed out loud at the sight.

Creating the world was such fun!
And that was the end of Day One.

Space floated with water, below and on high.
God parted the waters and spread out the sky.
And only the Son and the Spirit knew why.

Then God said, "There's much more to do.
But this is the end of Day Two."

"Let's hold back the waters and push up the land."
God fashioned, imagined each grain of the sand,
Formed flowers and fruit with a wave of His hand.

And all was as good as could be.
So that was the end of Day Three.

A hot ball of fire, God flung into space,
A silvery moon shining down on this place,
And millions of stars, flowing out of His grace.

"It's looking quite nice, but there's more."
And that was the end of Day Four.

God filled all the oceans with dolphins and whales,
Comical creatures with colorful scales.
Skies filled with songbirds, like sweet nightingales.

The earth was becoming alive.
And that was the end of Day Five.

Then God got creative, with camels and cats,
Zebras and weasels and beavers and bats,
Puppies and ponies and rabbits and rats.

But God wasn't finished, you know.
Day Six had a long way to go.

Next, Father and Son, with a plan they discussed,
Created a man out of nothing but dust.
They called the man "Adam" and asked for his trust.

God told him to name every pet.
Still, God wasn't finished just yet.

The man named his pets, but he still felt alone.
So God touched man's heart, as he took out one bone,
And fashioned for Adam a wife of his own.

"That's it!" Adam cried. "Eve's the one!"
And finally, Day Six was all done.

Day Seven, the Father and Son took a rest.
The Almighty God had created His best.
God honored Day Seven and called the day "blessed."

And that's how the earth was begun,
When God made the world with His Son.

Through his power all things were made—things in
heaven and on earth, things seen and unseen, all powers,
authorities, lords, and rulers. All things were made
through Christ and for Christ.

—Colossians 1:16